What Would **YOU Do?**

Should Bella Go to Bed?

Staying Healthy

Rebecca Rissman

Chicago, Illinois

To contact Capstone Global Library please phone 800-747-4992, or
visit our website www.capstonepub.com

Edited by Daniel Nunn, Rebecca Rissman, and Siân Smith
Designed by Steve Mead
Picture research by Mica Brancic
Production by Alison Parsons
Originated by Capstone Global Library Ltd
Printed and bound in China by Leo Paper Products Ltd

16 15 14 13 12
10 9 8 7 6 5 4 3 2 1

Library of Congress Cataloging-in-Publication Data
Rissman, Rebecca.
Should bella go to bed? : staying healthy / Rebecca Rissman.
  p. cm.—(What would you do?)
  Includes bibliographical references and index.
  ISBN 978-1-4329-7255-4 (hb)—ISBN 978-1-4329-7256-1 (pb) 1.
Health—Decision making—Juvenile literature. 2. Health behavior—
Juvenile literature.
I. Title. RA776.9 .R62 2013
  613—dc23   2012017436

Acknowledgments
All photographs © Capstone Publishers (Karon Dubke).

Every effort has been made to contact copyright holders of any
material reproduced in this book. Any omissions will be rectified in
subsequent printings if notice is given to the publisher.

Contents

Making Choices

We make choices every day, such as
"Should I eat healthy food?"

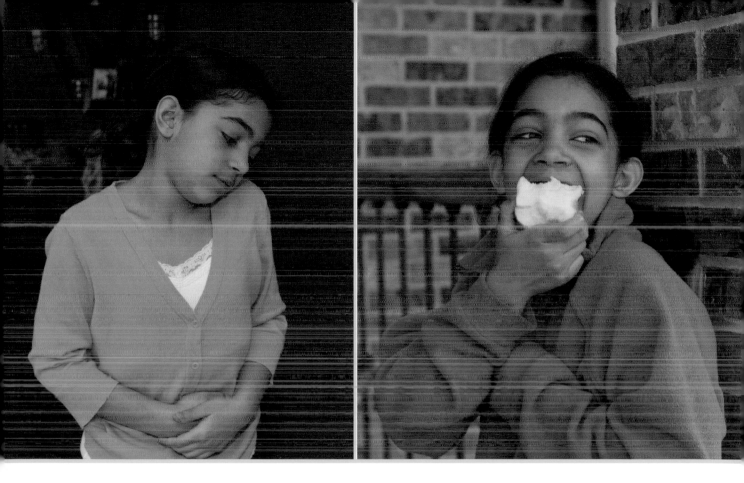

Our choices have effects.

Ask yourself if your choices will have good or bad effects.

Should Bella Go to Bed?

It is late. Should Bella go to bed?

Bella could choose to go to bed on time.

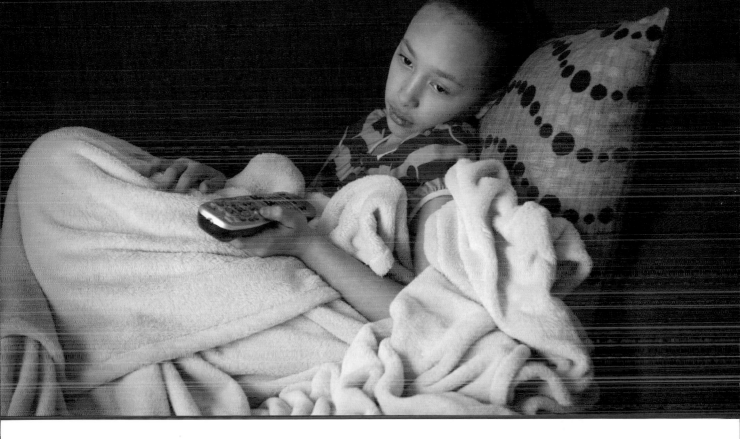

Bella could choose to stay up late.

What Would YOU Have Done?

If Bella had stayed up late, she may have felt tired and grumpy the next day. If Bella had gone to bed on time, she would have given her body the rest it needed for the next day.

Should Billy Play Outside?

It's a beautiful day. Should Billy play outside?

Billy could choose to play outside.

Billy could choose to watch television instead.

What Would YOU Have Done?

If Billy had played outside, the exercise would have helped his body and might have made him feel happy. If Billy had watched television instead, it might have made him feel tired or bored.

Should Charlotte Eat Healthy Food?

Charlotte has the choice of eating healthy food or unhealthy food. Which should Charlotte choose?

Charlotte could choose to eat
unhealthy food.

Charlotte could choose to eat healthy food.

What Would YOU Have Done?

If Charlotte always chose to eat unhealthy food, her body would not get what it needs to stay healthy and she could get ill. If Charlotte chose healthy food, it would help to keep her body fit and well.

Should Theo Tell an Adult?

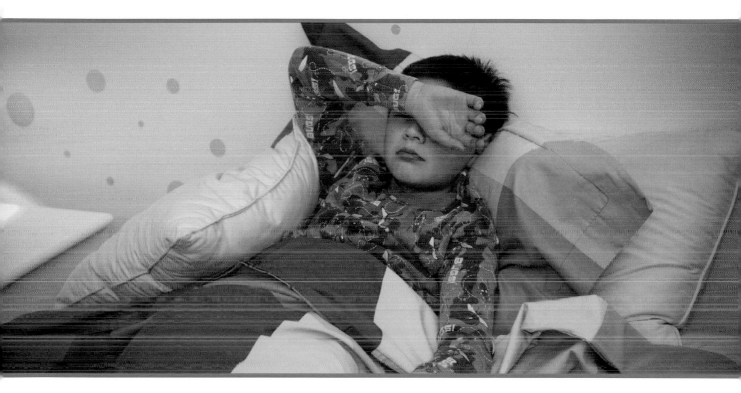

Theo wants to play with his friends but he feels ill. Should Theo tell his mother?

19

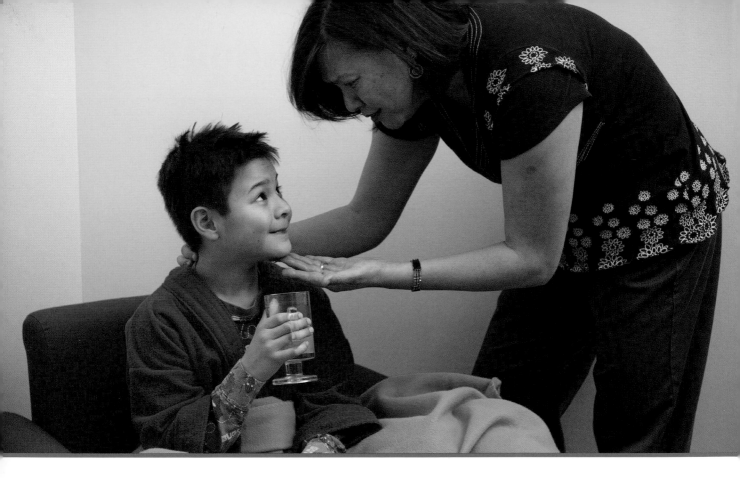

Theo could choose to tell his mother that he feels sick.

Theo could choose not to tell his
mother that he feels sick.

What Would YOU Have Done?

If Theo had told his mother that he felt sick, she could have given him medicine to make him feel better. If he did not tell his mother, his illness might have become worse and he could have made his friends sick, too.

Picture Glossary

choice a decision

effects the results of a decision or something you choose to do. Choices can have good or bad effects.

healthy food food that is good for your body

unhealthy food food that is not very good for your body. Unhealthy foods often have a lot of salt, sugar, or fat.

Index

Notes for Parents and Teachers

Before reading

Explain to children that there are consequences, or outcomes, for each of their decisions. Some outcomes are better than others. Ask children to reflect on a decision they made that day, for example, *what to eat for breakfast* or *what to wear to school*. Ask them to evaluate if the decision had a good outcome.

After reading

Ask children if they ever stay up past their bedtime. Then encourage children to record the outcome, or results, of their decision to stay awake longer than usual. Make a list of their responses. Then ask children how they feel when they go to bed on time. Make a list of these responses as well. Encourage children to compare the results of staying up late and going to bed on time. Which decision seems best to them?